Note to Librarians, Teachers, and Parents:

Blastoff! Readers are carefully developed by literacy experts and combine standards-based content with developmentally appropriate text.

Level 1 provides the most support through repetition of high-frequency words, light text, predictable sentence patterns, and strong visual support.

Level 2 offers early readers a bit more challenge through varied simple sentences, increased text load, and less repetition of high-frequency words.

Level 3 advances early-fluent readers toward fluency through increased text and concept load, less reliance on visuals, longer sentences, and more literary language.

Level 4 builds reading stamina by providing more text per page, increased use of punctuation, greater variation in sentence patterns, and increasingly challenging vocabulary.

Level 5 encourages children to move from "learning to read" to "reading to learn" by providing even more text, varied writing styles, and less familiar topics.

Whichever book is right for your reader, Blastoff! Readers are the perfect books to build confidence and encourage a love of reading that will last a lifetime!

This edition first published in 2017 by Bellwether Media, Inc.

No part of this publication may be reproduced in whole or in part without written permission of the publisher. For information regarding permission, write to Bellwether Media, Inc., Attention: Permissions Department, 5357 Penn Avenue South, Minneapolis, MN 55419.

Library of Congress Cataloging-in-Publication Data
Names: Schuh, Mari C., 1975- , author.
Title: Corals / by Mari Schuh.
Description: Minneapolis, MN : Bellwether Media, Inc., 2017. | Series: Blastoff! Readers. Ocean Life Up Close | Includes bibliographical references and index. | Audience: Ages 5 to 8. | Audience: Grades K to 3.
Identifiers: LCCN 2016035480 (print) | LCCN 2016042996 (ebook) | ISBN 9781626175693 (hardcover : alk. paper) | ISBN 9781681032900 (ebook)
Subjects: LCSH: Corals–Juvenile literature.
Classification: LCC QL377.C5 S37 2017 (print) | LCC QL377.C5 (ebook) | DDC 593.6–dc23
LC record available at https://lccn.loc.gov/2016035480

Text copyright © 2017 by Bellwether Media, Inc. BLASTOFF! READERS and associated logos are trademarks and/or registered trademarks of Bellwether Media, Inc. SCHOLASTIC, CHILDREN'S PRESS, and associated logos are trademarks and/or registered trademarks of Scholastic Inc.

Editor: Christina Leighton   Designer: Brittany McIntosh

Printed in the United States of America, North Mankato, MN.

Table of Contents

What Are Corals?	4
Kinds of Corals	8
Under the Sea	12
Coral Reefs	18
Glossary	22
To Learn More	23
Index	24

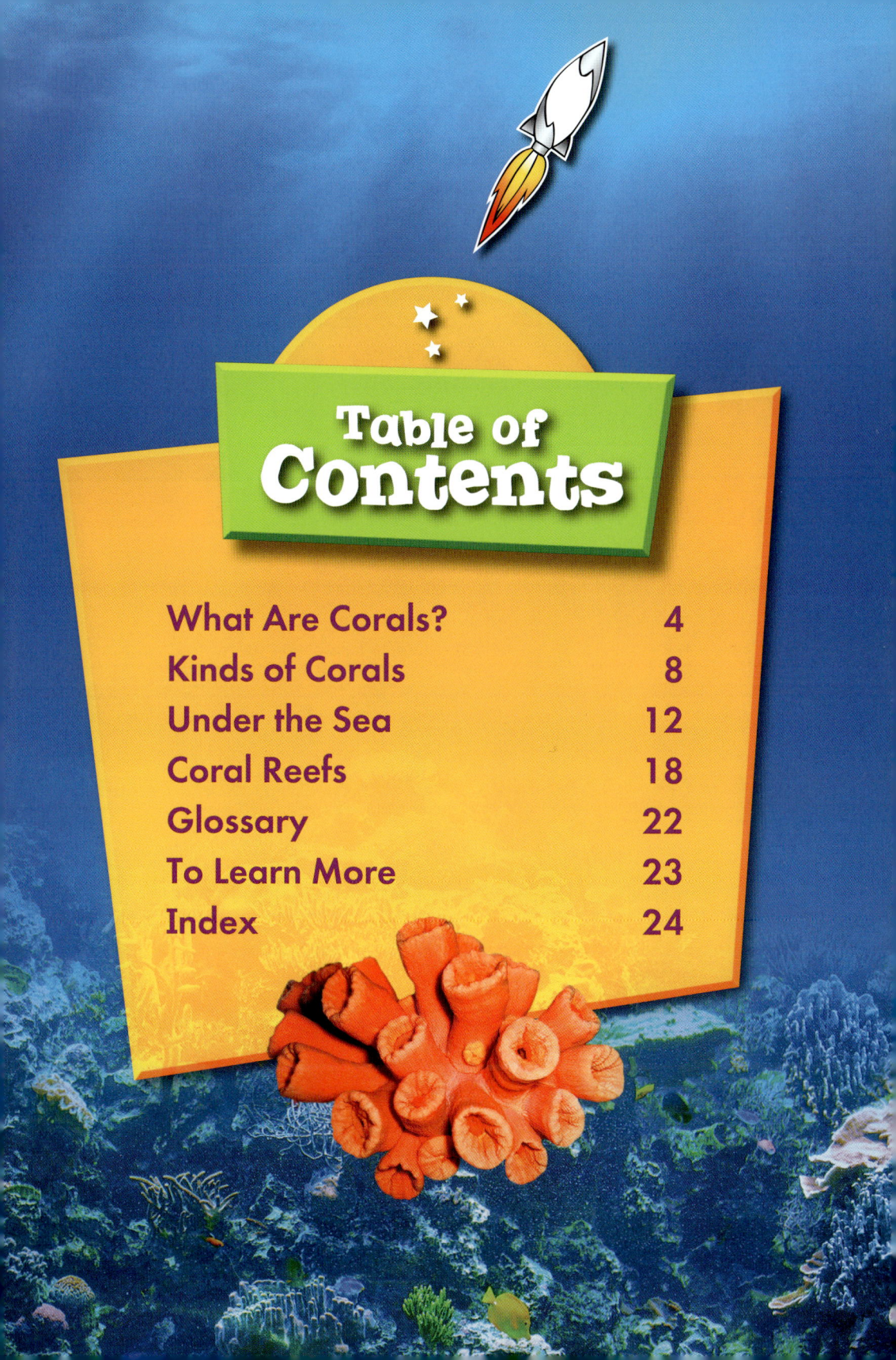

What Are Corals?

Corals look like plants or rocks under the sea. But these **invertebrates** are actually ocean animals!

Many corals live in warm, shallow water. Other kinds live in cool, deep water.

A coral is made up of a tiny, soft **polyp** and its **skeleton**. Corals often live together in **colonies**.

coral colony

A polyp is tube-shaped. **Tentacles** and a mouth are at the top of its body.

Kinds of Corals

Corals are many shapes, sizes, and colors. Soft corals have a skeleton inside their soft bodies.

sea whip

sea fan

Sea whips and sea fans are soft corals. Movement in the water can make them sway back and forth.

Hard corals have an outer skeleton that helps protect them from **predators**. They are also called stony corals.

Brain corals are a kind of hard coral. Their surface looks like a brain!

brain coral

Sea Enemies

bumphead parrotfish

crown-of-thorns sea star

foureye butterflyfish

Under the Sea

Algae live inside many types of coral. These tiny plants often give corals their different colors.

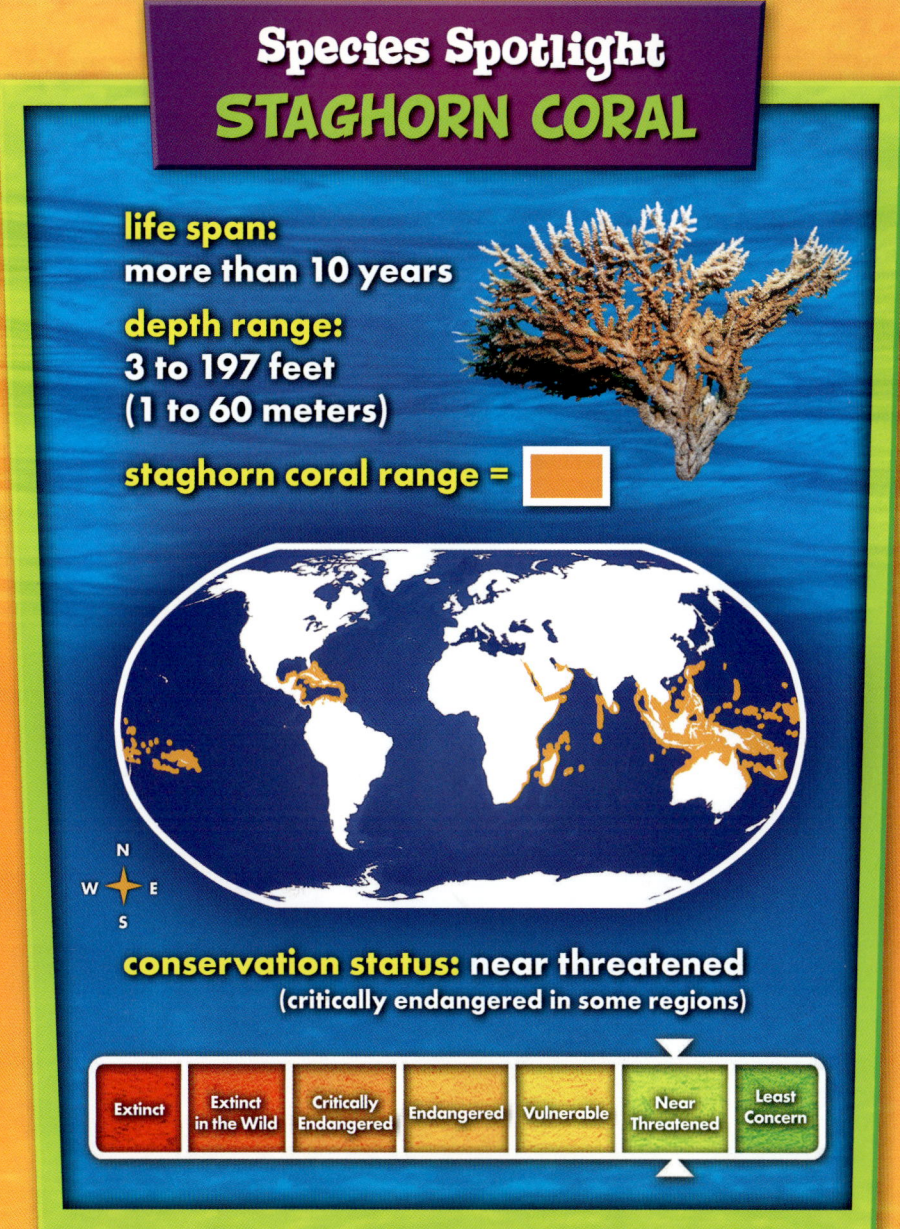

Algae provide **nutrients** and help corals grow. In return, the corals give algae a place to live.

Catch of the Day

zooplankton

green algae

cup corals

At night, some corals use their tentacles to eat. Their tentacles can sting and catch **prey**.

Corals sometimes eat **zooplankton**. They also grab small fish for a tasty meal.

Corals can form by **budding**. A part of the coral breaks off and grows into a new polyp.

egg

They also make new life by releasing many eggs. The eggs become **larvae**. Then they grow into polyps.

Coral Reefs

The world's amazing **coral reefs** are mostly made up of hard corals. Over time, the hard corals build on top of each other.

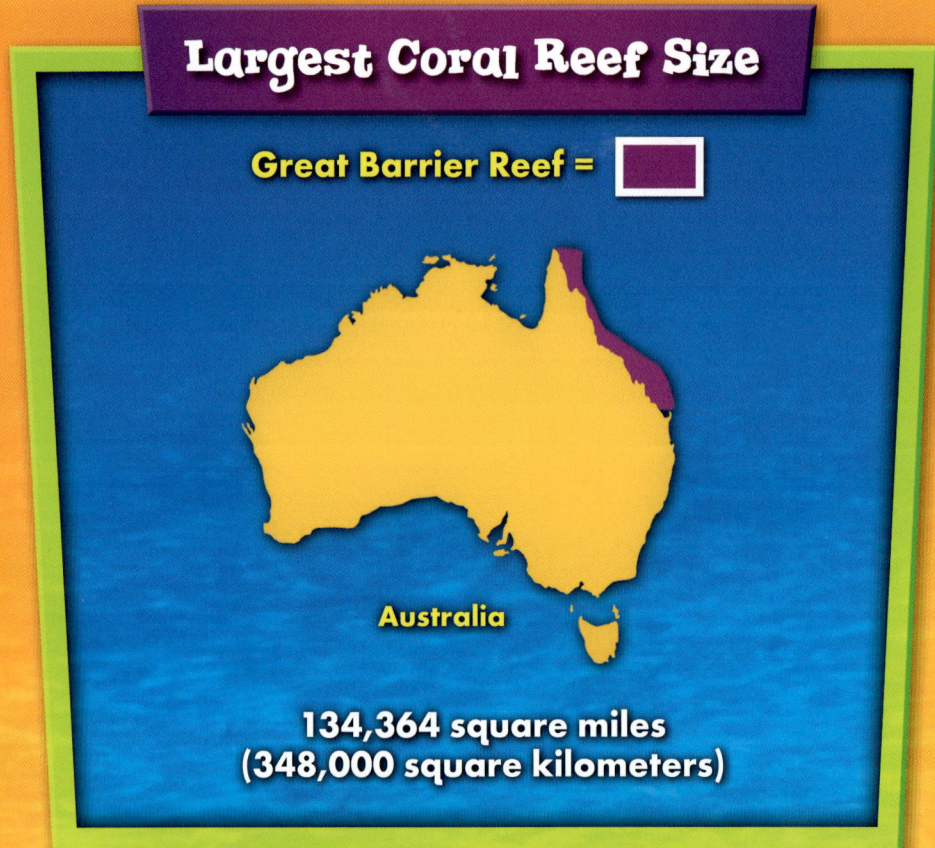

Largest Coral Reef Size

Great Barrier Reef =

Australia

134,364 square miles
(348,000 square kilometers)

The new corals form over the old skeletons. This makes the reef grow big!

Coral reefs are full of sea life. But too much fishing and other harmful events can hurt them.

People must help protect coral reefs. Corals are an important part of underwater communities!

Glossary

algae—plants and plantlike living things; most kinds of algae grow in water.

budding—when a piece of a coral polyp breaks off and becomes a new polyp; budding is one way coral polyps create new life.

colonies—groups of corals

coral reefs—structures made of coral that usually grow in shallow seawater

invertebrates—animals without backbones

larvae—early, tiny forms of an animal that must go through a big change to become adults

nutrients—substances that are needed for growth and healthy living

polyp—an animal that has a tube-shaped body and is attached to a hard place

predators—animals that hunt other animals for food

prey—animals that are hunted by other animals for food

skeleton—the bones that support an animal's body

tentacles—long, bendable parts of a coral polyp that are attached to the body

zooplankton—ocean animals that drift in water; most zooplankton are tiny.

To Learn More

AT THE LIBRARY
Heos, Bridget. *Do You Really Want to Visit a Coral Reef?* Mankato, Minn.: Amicus, 2015.

Kopp, Megan. *What Do You Find in a Coral Reef?* New York, N.Y.: Crabtree Publishing Company, 2016.

Schuetz, Kari. *Life in a Coral Reef.* Minneapolis, Minn.: Bellwether Media, 2016.

ON THE WEB
Learning more about corals is as easy as 1, 2, 3.

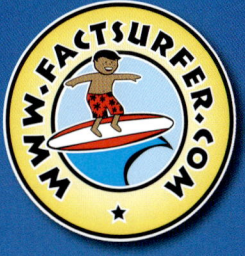

1. Go to www.factsurfer.com.

2. Enter "corals" into the search box.

3. Click the "Surf" button and you will see a list of related web sites.

With factsurfer.com, finding more information is just a click away.

Index

algae, 12, 13, 14
body, 7, 8
budding, 16
colonies, 6
colors, 8, 12
coral reefs, 18, 19, 20, 21
depth, 13
eat, 15
eggs, 16, 17
invertebrates, 4
larvae, 17
life span, 13
mouth, 7
nutrients, 13
polyp, 6, 7, 16, 17
predators, 10, 11
prey, 14, 15
protect, 10, 21
range, 13

shapes, 7, 8
sizes, 8, 18, 19
skeleton, 6, 8, 10, 19
status, 13
tentacles, 7, 15

The images in this book are reproduced through the courtesy of: Jolanta Wojcicka, front cover; Khoroshunova Olga, p. 3; sergemi, pp. 4, 12; bearacreative, p. 5; metha1819, p. 6; Jung Hsuan, p. 7 (top left); John A. Anderson, pp. 7 (top center, top right), 9; Frolova_Elena, p. 7 (bottom); Fiona Ayerst, p. 8; Natursports, p. 10; SeraphP, p. 11 (top left); tae208, p. 11 (top center); Jeremy Brown, p. 11 (top right); Sphinx Wang, p. 11 (bottom); Richard Whitcombe, p. 13; Lebendkulturen.de, p. 14 (top left); Aleksandar Mijatovic, p. 14 (top right); Ron and Valerie Taylor/ ardea.c/ Pantheon/ SuperStock, p. 14 (bottom); Jeff Rotman/ Exactostock-1598/ SuperStock, p. 15; Tim Rock/ Polaris/ Newscom, pp. 16, 17 (top); Age Fotostock/ SuperStock, p. 17 (bottom left); FLPA/ D P Wilson/ Age Fotostock, p. 17 (bottom right); ifish, p. 19; melissaf84, pp. 20-21.

593.6 S　　　　　　　　　　　　**FLT**
Schuh, Mari C.,
Corals /

08/17